MARRIAGE SURVIVAL

SECRET

*Top-Most Secret to having a Happy,
Successful and Healthy Marriage among
Newly Wedded Couples*

Callie Bright

TABLE OF CONTENTS

INTRODUCTION

WHAT IS MARRIAGE?

Marriage According to the Law and Local Custom

REASON WHY YOU MUST BE MARRIED

EIGHT ESSENTIAL BENEFITS OF HAVING A HAPPY AND HEALTHY MARRIAGE

Love and commitment.

Being faithful in bed.

Humility.

Time.

Honesty and Trust

Good Communication

Selflessness.

MARRIAGE SURVIVAL SECRET

Keep a constant focus on each other's best qualities.

Make the conscious decision to find your partner attractive.

Keep the humor flowing.

Have fun and enjoy yourselves together.

Happy couples argue

If you're waiting for your partner to be ultimately you, they probably won't.

Enjoy life's little pleasures.

Respect and appreciate each other

Learn to adapt to new situations.

Treat each other with compassion

INTRODUCTION

Marriage as we know is a social organization that has been around for centuries. It is a legal contract between two people who are in a relationship and want to be together for the rest of their lives. Marriage is a way to protect the couple's assets and ensure that both will take care of them. Marriage is also a legally and socially sanctioned union, usually between a man and a woman. It is regulated by-laws, rules, customs, beliefs, and attitudes that prescribe the rights and duties of the partners, and it accords status to their offspring which would be discussed in full in this book.

It is generally known that marriage in contemporary times has been debated in many different contexts worldwide. Couples who once loved each other are now losing interest in one another. This is simply because they did not know the secret that could make their relationship last longer at the beginning of the wedding or while they were dating because they did not know the secret that can make their relationship last longer. This is because they were unaware of the key factor that may have contributed to the longevity of their relationship. This book will give a lot of knowledge on cultivating a pleasant, fruitful, and healthful marriage connection with your partner or spouse, and it will do it in a wholesome way. READ and make the most out of the experience

WHAT IS MARRIAGE?

Marriage is a social organization that has been around for centuries. It is a legal contract between two people who are in a relationship and want to be together forever. Marriage is a way to protect the couple's assets and ensure that both will take care of them if something happens to one of them. Marriage is also a legally and socially sanctioned union, usually between a man and a woman. It is regulated by laws, rules, customs, beliefs, and attitudes that prescribe the rights and duties of the partners, and it accords status to their offspring. Marriage is typically between a man and a woman (if any). It is possible to attribute the prevalence of marriage across various societies and cultures to the numerous fundamental social and personal functions for which it provides structure. These functions include sexual gratification and regulation, the division of labor between the sexes, economic production and consumption, and the satisfaction of personal needs for affection, status, and companionship. The regulation of lines of descent, the care of children, their education and socialization, and the act of procreation are perhaps the essential functions. Marriage has emerged in a wide variety of different forms throughout human history.

MARRIAGE ACCORDING TO THE LAW AND LOCAL CUSTOM

In every human society, whether ancient or modern, marriage has been observed. The intricate legal framework and traditions that surround it attest to its significance. Laws and rituals are as diverse and numerous as the societies and cultures in which humans live.

The primary legal role of marriage is to secure the rights of spouses concerning both of them and to ensure the rights and define the connections of children within society. Tradition says that a child born into a legal marriage has the right to inherit and other rights that the community has set up. In most countries, a union determines if a couple can have children and what kind of relationship they can have with their children, including whom they can marry.

Until this century, marriage was rarely a question of personal choice. In Western countries, love between spouses came to be linked with marriage, although even in Western romantic love was not the primary incentive for matrimony in most ages, and one carefully chose one's marital partner.

The earliest social restriction regarding marriage is endogamy or the practice of marrying within one's tribe or community. Endogamous marriage occurs naturally in societies when contact with other communities is difficult or nonexistent. Some communities still put a lot of pressure on people to marry within their own social, economic, and ethnic groups.

In communities with complicated family networks, large groups of people who share a common ancestor are often forbidden from marrying inside their group, a practice known as exogamy.

Parents traditionally arrange marriages in cultures where the extended family plays a central role. There is a lot of thought into how the match might help the extended family socially and financially, with the hope that love will grow between the couples after the wedding. In contrast, young people often make their own mating decisions in countries where the nuclear family is the norm. It has been considered that love precedes (and decides) marriage, and less emphasis is generally given to the socio-economic components of the relationship.

In civilizations with planned marriages, the universal norm is that someone acts as a mediator or matchmaker. This person's principal task is to arrange a marriage agreeable to the two families represented. Some type of dowry or bridewealth is nearly always exchanged in communities that promote arranged weddings.

⍰

REASON WHY YOU MUST BE MARRIED

1. ## IT IS SECURE AND SAFE

   Men and women have a reduced risk of becoming domestic violence victims when married. According to a report published by the Justice Department in 1994 and derived from the National Crime Victimization Survey, divorced women and single women have a four to five times greater risk of becoming victims of violent crime in any given year than married women. Additionally, single men have a four times greater risk of becoming victims of violent crime than married men. Two-thirds of violent acts committed against women by intimate partners were not carried out by the women's husbands but rather by boyfriends (whether live-in or not) or by men who had previously been the women's husbands or boyfriends. According to the findings of the relevant studies, one researcher summarizes the findings as follows: "Regardless of methodology, the studies had shown similar results: unmarried people that are staying together engage in more violence than spouses." In preparation for the publication of our new book, Linda Waite analyzed data from the National Survey of Families and Households. She found that persons who live together are three times more likely than married couples to report that their disputes got violent (such as kicking, hitting, or shoving) in the preceding year. The issue was the case even after adjusting for demographics such as education, race, age, and gender.

2.   SAVE YOUR LIFE:

People who get married tend to live healthier and longer lives. When one is in their late middle years, one sees the power of marriage particularly clearly. For example, Linda Waite and a colleague found an astonishingly large "marriage gap" in longevity when they analyzed mortality differentials in an extensive, nationally representative sample: nine out of ten married guys who are alive at around 40+ will make it to age 70, whereas only six out of ten comparable single guys will make it to age 65. (controlling for race, education, and income). The protective benefits of marriage are also substantial for women, though they are not quite as large as they are for men. In comparison, only eight out of ten divorced or single women will make it to their senior years if they are still alive at the age of 48, but nine out of ten wives will.

One of the most significant dangers individuals willingly put themselves through is the chance of not being married—a comparison of relative mortality risks. For example, a man's life expectancy can be cut by just under six years if he suffers from heart disease; however, a man's life can be cut by almost ten years if he is never married. This is not just an options effect: even when controlling for initial health status, Married persons have a higher survival rate while ill than their single counterparts. This is true even when controlling for initial health status. Having a spouse lowers a cancer patient's risk of dying by as much as being in a ten-year younger age group. Researchers have shown that married people have a lower chance of dying in the hospital than single people. A recent study examining surgical patients' outcomes found that a patient's risk of dying while in the hospital was reduced just because they were married. If a patient was unmarried, there was a 2.5 times greater chance that they would be discharged from the hospital and placed in a nursing home than married. This may be due to more obvious reasons. Researchers who have conducted studies on the function of the immune system in the laboratory have discovered that happily married couples have immune systems that function better. Even many years after the divorce, people who have been through a divorce show much lower levels of immune function.

3.   SAVE THE LIVES OF YOUR CHILDREN

If parents marry and remain married, their children have longer, healthier lives. Adults who worry about passive smoking and impaired driving would do well to pay at least some attention to this issue. A parent's divorce reduced the adult child's life expectancy by four years in one long-term study that followed a group of highly advantaged children (middle-class whites with IQs of at least 135) up to their seventies. Compared to 40-year-olds whose parents remained married, 40-year-olds from divorced homes had a threefold greater risk of dying from any cause.

4.   YOU WILL MAKE MORE MONEY

Men today view marriage as a luxury item and a financial burden. Nonetheless, a vast and extensive body of scientific literature demonstrates that for men, in particular, marriage is a productive institution—as crucial as education for increasing a man's income. Marriage may improve an American man's earnings roughly the same as a college degree. According to some estimates, married men earn 40 percent more than equivalent unmarried men, even after controlling for education and employment experience. The longer a man remains married, the greater his marriage premium. Wives also gain from marriage, but their earnings decrease when motherhood enters the scene. White wives without children receive a 4 percent marital salary premium, but black wives earn 10 percent more than equivalent single women.

5.   DID I MENTION THAT YOU'LL MAKE A LOT MORE MONEY?

People who are married not only make more money but also spend it better and save more than they would if they were single. At the same income level, married people are less likely to say they are in "economic hardship" or have trouble paying essential bills. The longer you are matched with your partner, the more assets you build. On the other hand, the length of a relationship has nothing to do with how much money you have. At the point of retirement, the average married couple has saved about $410,000. This is compared to $167,000 for people who have never been married and $154,000 for people who have been divorced. In one study, the assets of married couples grew twice as fast as those of divorced couples over five years.

6. YOU WOULD BE ABLE TO CONTROL YOUR PARTNER'S CHEATING HEART

Marriage makes people more faithful in bed. Men who live with their wives are four times more likely to cheat than husbands, and women who live with their husbands are eight times more likely to cheat than wives. Marriage is the only natural way to ensure a romantic relationship will last. After five years, only one out of ten couples who live together are still living together. On the other hand, 80 percent of couples who get married for the first time are still married after five years, and if current divorce rates stay the same, close to 60 percent will remain married for life. One British study found that biological parents who get married are three times more likely to still be together two years later than biological parents who live together. This was true even after considering the mother's age, education, financial problems, failed relationships in the past, depression, and the quality of the relationship. Marriage may be riskier than it used to be, but there is still no better way to make love last.

7. YOU WON'T LOSE YOUR MIND

Getting married is good for your mind. Married Partners are less likely to be depressed, anxious, or mentally upset than single, divorced, or widowed. Divorce, on the other hand, hurts both men's and women's mental health, making them more depressed and angry and lowering their sense of self-worth, mastery, and purpose in life.

And this isn't just a statistical trick. Careful researchers who have followed people as they move toward marriage have found that it's not just that happy, healthy people get married, but that getting married significantly boosts their mental health. In the late 1980s and early 1990s, Nadine Marks and James Lambert looked at how the mental health of a large group of Americans changed. They started by measuring people's mental health and then watched what happened to them over the next few years as they married, stayed single, or split up. When people get married, their mental health is always greatly improved. When people got divorced, their mental and emotional health got a lot worse. For example, their depression got worse, and they were less happy. People who got divorced during this time also felt less in control of their lives, had less positive relationships with others, felt less like they had a purpose in life, and were less accepting of themselves than their married peers.

Men who are married are only half as likely to kill themselves as single men and one-third as likely as divorced men. Wives are also much less likely to kill themselves than women who are single, divorced, or who have lost a partner. Married people are much less likely to drink too much or use illegal drugs. In a recent national survey, one in four single men between the ages of 19 and 26 said that drinking makes them aggressive at work or home. Only one in seven married men in the same period said the same thing.

8.   YOU WILL BE GLAD TO DO IT.

Most people overestimate the remarkable things about being single or getting a divorce. Overall, 40% of married people say they are "pleased" with life, while only 25% of single people or people who live with someone else say the same. About half as many married people as single people or people who live with someone else say they are unhappy with their lives.

How happy are divorced people? People often say that people get divorced to be satisfied, but if that's true, most should ask for their money back. Only 18% of divorced adults say they are "pleased," and they are twice as likely to say they generally are not too happy with life in general as married people. Only a small number of adults who get divorced end up in new relationships that are better than the ones they left. Some cultural voices say, "Divorce or be miserable," but the truth is that "divorce and be miserable" is at least as likely to happen.

This isn't just happening in the United States. Steven Stack and J. Ross Eshleman looked at 17 developed countries and found that "married people are much happier than single people." This was true even when they considered gender, age, education, children, church attendance, financial satisfaction, and self-reported health. Also, "the link between being married and being happy is powerful and stays the same across nations." Marriage improved both financial happiness and health. But being married made people happier in ways that went beyond improving their finances and health. Cohabitation, on the other hand, didn't improve financial satisfaction or how healthy people thought they were. Having a live-in lover also didn't make people as happy as getting married. In an extensive study of 100,000 Norwegians, "the married have the highest level of subjective well-being, followed by the widowed," for both men and women. Even people who divorced for a long time but still lived together were not happier than single people.

9.   YOUR CHILDREN WILL LOVE YOU MORE

In the long run, divorce makes it harder for parents and children to stay close to each other. On average, adult children of divorce say less good things about their relationships with their mother and father, and they are about 40% less likely to say they see either parent at least several times a week than adults from intact marriages.

10.   YOU WILL HAVE A BETTER SEXUAL LIFE

Even though the sex in the City ads promise singles untold erotic joys, both husbands and wives are likelier to say that their sex lives are very satisfying than singles or people who live with others. Divorced women were alleged to have sexual energy that made them feel emotionally fulfilled. One reason is that married people are more likely to have a sexual life. Compared to married people, single men are 20 times more likely, and single women are ten times likely not to have had sex in the past year. (Nearly a quarter of single men and 30% of single women don't have sexual partners.)

Married people are also most likely to say that their sex lives are very satisfying. For example, wives are almost twice as likely as divorced or never-married women to have a sex life that a) exists and b) is very emotionally satisfying. Contrary to what most people outside there think, having a wife is much better for men than living together: 50 percent of husbands say that having sex with their partner is very physically satisfying, while only 39 percent of men who live together say the same.

EIGHT ESSENTIAL BENEFITS OF HAVING A HAPPY AND HEALTHY MARRIAGE

1. **LOVE AND COMMITMENT.**

    At its heart, love is a choice to be loyal to someone else. It is much more than a fleeting feeling, as shown on TV, in movies, and romance books. Feelings come and go, but a natural decision to stay together is forever, making a marriage healthy.

    Marriage is a choice to stick with someone through the good and bad times. When things are going well, it's easy to stick with something. But true love shows itself by staying together even when life is hard.

2. **BEING FAITHFUL IN BED.**

    There is more to sexual faithfulness in a marriage than just our bodies. It also includes our eyes, minds, hearts, and souls. When we spend much time thinking about how we would like to be sexual with someone else, we give up being sexually faithful to our partner. When we let another person get close to us emotionally, we give up being sexually faithful to our partner.

    Protect your sexuality every day and give it all to your partner. Sexual faithfulness requires self-control and knowing what will happen if you break your promise. Don't let anything near your eyes, body, or heart that would make you less faithful.

3. **HUMILITY.**

    We all have flaws, and relationships show these flaws more quickly than anything else. A healthy marriage needs both partners to be able to admit that they are not perfect, will make mistakes, and will need forgiveness. Being better than your partner will make them feel bad about themselves and stop your relationship from getting better.

    If you have trouble with this, grab a pencil and quickly write down three things your partner does better than you. This simple task should help you stay unpretentious. Repeat this as many times as you can.

4. **SPNDING MUCH TIME TOGETHER**

    Relationships fail when people don't put effort into them. I never have and I never will. Quality time together should be a priority in every relationship. When time is limited, it's hard to have significant interactions.

    Your marriage should be the closest and most meaningful connection you have. Therefore, couples will need more time than in any other relationship. Try to schedule regular alone time with your partner. And it wouldn't hurt to have a date night every once in a while.

5. **PATIENCE AND FORGIVENESS.**

    Patience and forgiveness are always necessary for marriage because neither partner is flawless. Successful spouses learn to forgive and tolerate one another no matter what. They recognize their own fallibility and have realistic expectations of their spouse. They don't try to hold their partner captive by dredging up the past.

To add insult to injury, they don't try to put things proper or exact revenge when things go wrong. If you are holding onto a past pain from your lover, forgive him or her. It will set your heart and relationship free.

6. HONESTY AND TRUST

In a successful marriage, honesty and trust become the bedrock on which all else is built. However, unlike most items on this list, trust takes time to develop. You can instantly become selfless, devoted, and patient, but building trust takes time. Only after weeks, months, and years of being who you say you are and doing what you say you'll do is trust established. It takes time, so begin immediately, and if you need to reestablish trust in your relationship, you will have to work even more challenging.

7. GOOD COMMUNICATION

In a happy marriage, the couple talks to one other frequently. They talk about the kids' schedules, shopping lists, and bills. However, that's not all they do. They also express their emotions, including happiness, sadness, worry, and excitement. They talk about the emotional growth they're experiencing alongside the kid and the physical growth the kid is experiencing.

Since open and frank exchanges lay the groundwork for virtues such as dedication, tolerance, and trust, partners cannot ignore them.

8.   SELFLESSNESS.

More marriages end in divorce due to selfishness than any other cause, but one will never measure this. Many surveys attribute it to money problems, a lack of commitment, cheating, or an overall lack of compatibility, but the truth is that selfishness is at the heart of most of these issues. A selfish person cares only about themselves, is impatient with others, and never develops the skills necessary to be a good partner in a marriage. The best way to make your lover happy is to give them your dreams and life so that you can start your new life together.

This is just a kind reminder to give your spouse plenty of attention and make everyday efforts to strengthen your union.

If you want to be living together to be very happy and long-lasting, you will have to put in much work, but it will be worth it.

A happy, healthy marriage is far more critical than most of the fleeting things we strive for in this life. And they always outlast the rest.

[?]

MARRIAGE SURVIVAL SECRET

Weddings are much fun with dancing and laughter, but being married isn't always a walk in the park either. (Occasionally, it's more like the lump of icing that went up to your nose when you were smashing it; you had excellent motives, but the product was not what you wanted.) It takes much effort to genuinely live "blissfully ever after," so whether you've been married for decades or just got married. We asked the professionals for advice on what steps married couples should take to improve their chances of a successful marriage. Consider their helpful recommendations if you want your relationship to be stronger, better, and even more pleasurable.

KEEP A CONSTANT FOCUS ON EACH OTHER'S BEST QUALITIES.

It is not always simple to look beyond little annoyances, and there may be occasions when you actively despise your spouse. However, according to Ellen Chute, LMSW, to have a successful marriage, you need to establish realistic expectations for yourself and accept the strengths and shortcomings of your partner. For instance, if you're better with numbers, you shouldn't get furious when they mess up the checkbook's balance. By the way, it would be better if you had made it your responsibility to determine the budget. Instead of managing meal planning, they may focus on their strength, which may be cooking. According to Suzann Pileggi Pawelski, co-author of the book Happy Together, which she authored with her husband, James Pawelski, Ph.D., "using our abilities daily is related to increased well-being." The pair wrote the book together. "And when we assist our spouse in utilizing their talents, we feel more relational happiness,"

MAKE THE CONSCIOUS DECISION TO FIND YOUR PARTNER ATTRACTIVE.

You have the power to decide whether or not your mate is attractive. Yes, whether you believe it or not. According to Sunny McMillan, a professional life coach, radio broadcaster, and author of the book Unhitched, "Attraction to your spouse is something that you have the authority to make throughout your marriage." She advises engaging in what she calls "attraction thoughts." She recommends concentrating on the qualities of your partner that most attract you, such as the length of your spouse's legs or how they raise your children (this trait need not be physical). The great news is that to be attracted to your partner. They do not need to have a career as a cover model. "Happy marriages are built on a sense of connection," Chute says. "Appeal on a physical level goes far deeper than superficial appearances."

KEEP THE HUMOR FLOWING.

Finding humor amid difficulty is a survival skill; life is complicated. Morris adds that a couple with a sense of humor is more likely to be able to work through difficult times together and that he advises all couples to learn to laugh at themselves. She claims to have seen that partners in healthy marriages are naturally comfortable with one another. She argues that you may achieve a stronger connection with your partner via shared laughing, be it inside jokes, a funny text message, or even just watching your favorite comedy together.

HAVE FUN AND ENJOY YOURSELVES TOGETHER.

Sharing experiences is essential to a good marriage, but neither spouse should become too dependent on the other. Pawelski argues that partners may strengthen a couple's bond by sharing common hobbies outside of their typical routine.

When partners develop a common interest and pursue it together (via, say, a cooking class or tennis lessons), they grow as a unit. Morris claims that the hallmark of a happy partnership is shared enthusiasm for life. These shared experiences strengthen their bond, whether they've had a passion for travel, a strong desire to start a family, or a devotion to an exact cause.

HAPPY COUPLES ARGUE

True bliss in matrimony is a myth. "In a relationship, there is always misunderstanding," explains psychotherapist Erica MacGregor. But she adds that the couples in successful marriages know how to heal their arguments by listening to one other's side and recognizing when the conversation has veered off track. Family and couples therapist Dr. Juliana Morris notes that some of the happiest couples she has dealt with "had endured bad times." So, just because you and your spouse have disagreements from time to time or are experiencing a hard patch does not imply that your marriage is miserable. It probably tells you you're normal.

IF YOU'RE WAITING FOR YOUR PARTNER TO BE ULTIMATELY YOU, THEY PROBABLY WON'T.

Jerry Maguire is just a fictional figure, after all. It was amazing when he said, "You complete me," but it wouldn't work in everyday life. According to Pawelski, an unhealthy relationship is one in which both partners cannot develop as individuals because they depend on one another for their happiness. Instead of trying to "complete" one another, she believes, good couples should "complement" one another. We should be confident, self-aware, and complete before approaching another individual. Instead of wanting a partner to fill the vacuum, focus on yourself by enrolling in a class you're interested in and scheduling time to get out with friends.

ENJOY LIFE'S LITTLE PLEASURES.

Most people know the significance of supporting one's partner during adversity. However, Palwelski stresses the importance of remembering positive experiences as well. According to her, relationships have more positive than negative occurrences, but partners seldom take advantage of them. Therefore, "immediately stop what you're doing and devote your complete attention" the next time your partner communicates something nice, such as a compliment from their employer. Help them soak in the excellent news by encouraging them to ask questions and join the party. Doing so is a way of expressing appreciation for the good times shared in your marriage.

RESPECT AND APPRECIATE EACH OTHER

When you spend a lot of time with someone, it's easy to take them for granted. But MacGregor says you should tell them daily how much you appreciate them. "We all need to feel appreciated and reaffirmed for what we are doing right," says MacGregor. You can do this by pointing out something nice they did or telling them something you like about them. For example, if your partner makes you tea every morning, tell them that it made you smile and gave you an excellent start to the day. "If we don't feel like we're important, we might get angry and grow apart.

LEARN TO ADAPT TO NEW SITUATIONS.

When it comes to marital bliss, Pawelski thinks that both partners need to be open to change. She explains that people's wants and needs shift as they mature and form new connections with others. What we require now may be obsolete in the future. Morris concurs: She stresses the lack of a flexible, balanced dance between partners. For the simple reason that a happy marriage requires two people who are committed to each other's development as individuals and as a unit to work together for their mutual success. Your wedding will last long.

TREAT EACH OTHER WITH COMPASSION

"It's vital to be courteous and understanding of your spouse," says MacGregor. Criticizing and judging others leads to defensiveness and bitterness, as the saying goes. If you want to preserve the peace in your marriage, you should avoid personal attacks on your mate whenever possible. For instance, she advises against the remark, "you're such a slob!" You never do the dishes! Instead, try saying something like, "Because I prepared supper, I'd love it if you could wash the dishes tonight." Sound how much better that is?

Printed in Great Britain
by Amazon